THE ARDEN SHAKESPEARE
BOOK OF QUOTATIONS

ON

Life

Compiled by
JANE ARMSTRONG

AS

The Arden website is at
http://www.ardenshakespeare.com

First published 2001 by The Arden Shakespeare

This Collection Copyright © 2001 Jane Armstrong

Arden Shakespeare is an imprint of Thomson Learning

Thomson Learning
Berkshire House
168–173 High Holborn
London WC1V 7AA

Designed and typeset by Martin Bristow

Printed in Singapore by Seng Lee Press

All rights reserved. No part of this book may be printed
or reproduced or utilised in any form or by any
electronic, mechanical or other means, now known or
hereafter invented, including photocopying and
recording, or in any information storage or retrieval
system, without permission in writing from the
publishers.

British Library Cataloguing in Publication Data
A catalogue record for this book is available from the
British Library

Library of Congress Cataloguing in Publication Data
A catalogue record has been requested

ISBN 1-903436-51-6

NPN 9 8 7 6 5 4 3 2 1

THE ARDEN SHAKESPEARE
BOOKS OF QUOTATIONS

Life

Love

Death

Nature

Songs & Sonnets

The Seven Ages of Man

Ourselves

If our virtues
Did not go forth of us, 'twere all alike
As if we had them not.

Measure for Measure 1.1.33–5

No man is the lord of anything,
Though in and of him there be much consisting,
Till he communicate his parts to others.

Troilus and Cressida 3.3.117–19

'Tis the mind that makes the body rich.

Taming of the Shrew 4.3.170

Our bodies are gardens, to the which our wills
are gardeners.

Othello 1.3.322–3

Men's faults do seldom to themselves appear.

Lucrece 633

Happy are they that hear their detractions and can
put them to mending.

Much Ado About Nothing 2.3.220–1

How would you be
If He, which is the top of judgement, should
But judge you as you are?

Measure for Measure 2.2.75–7

Poor soul, the centre of my sinful earth,
Feeding these rebel powers that thee array,
Why dost thou pine within and suffer dearth,
Painting thy outward walls so costly gay?
Why so large cost, having so short a lease,
Dost thou upon thy fading mansion spend?
Shall worms, inheritors of this excess,
Eat up thy charge? Is this thy body's end?
Then soul, live thou upon thy servant's loss,
And let that pine to aggravate thy store;
Buy terms divine in selling hours of dross,
Within be fed, without be rich no more:
    So shalt thou feed on death, that feeds on men,
    And death once dead, there's no more dying then.

Sonnet 146

Simply the thing I am
Shall make me live.

All's Well That Ends Well 4.3.327–8

What piece of work is a man, how noble in reason, how infinite in faculties, in form and moving how express and admirable, in action how like an angel, in apprehension how like a god: the beauty of the world, the paragon of animals – and yet, to me, what is this quintessence of dust? Man delights not me – nor woman neither, though by your smiling you seem to say so.

Hamlet 2.2.305–12

What is a man
If his chief good and market of his time
Be but to sleep and feed?

Hamlet 4.4.33–5

Thou art the thing itself. Unaccommodated man is no more but such a poor, bare, forked animal as thou art.

King Lear 3.4.105–7

TROUBLES

O time, thou must untangle this, not I,
It is too hard a knot for me to untie.

Twelfth Night 2.2.40–1

There's something in his soul
O'er which his melancholy sits on brood.

Hamlet 3.1.165–6

I have of late, but wherefore I know not, lost all my
mirth, forgone all custom of exercises; and indeed it
goes so heavily with my disposition that this goodly
frame the earth seems to me a sterile promontory,
this most excellent canopy the air, look you, this brave
o'erhanging firmament, this majestical roof fretted
with golden fire, why, it appeareth nothing to me
but a foul and pestilent congregation of vapours.

Hamlet 2.2.297–305

By my troth Nerissa, my little body is aweary of this great world.

Merchant of Venice 1.2.1–2

All's cheerless, dark and deadly.

King Lear 5.3.288

There's nothing in this world can make me joy:
Life is as tedious as a twice-told tale
Vexing the dull ear of a drowsy man.

King John 3.3.107–9

My mind is troubled, like a fountain stirred,
And I myself see not the bottom of it.

Troilus and Cressida 3.3.310–11

When sorrows come, they come not single spies,
But in battalions.

Hamlet 4.5.78–9

O ye gods, ye gods, must I endure all this?

Julius Caesar 4.3.41

The worst is not
So long as we can say 'This is the worst.'

King Lear 4.1.29–30

To fear the worst oft cures the worse.

Troilus and Cressida 3.2.71

I am not prone to weeping . . . but I have
That honourable grief lodged here which burns
Worse than tears drown.

Winter's Tale 2.1.108–12

Every one can master a grief but he that has it.

Much Ado About Nothing 3.2.26–7

Let grief
Convert to anger; blunt not the heart, enrage it.

Macbeth 4.3.228–9

Give sorrow words; the grief, that does not speak,
Whispers the o'er-fraught heart, and bids it break.

Macbeth 4.3.209–10

Things without all remedy
Should be without regard: what's done is done.

Macbeth 3.2.11–12

Certainties . . . are past remedies.

Cymbeline 1.7.96–7

What's gone and what's past help
Should be past grief.

Winter's Tale 3.2.220–1

Be patient, for the world is broad and wide.

Romeo and Juliet 3.3.16

VIRTUE

That light we see is burning in my hall:
How far that little candle throws his beams!
So shines a good deed in a naughty world.

Merchant of Venice 5.1.89–91

Never anything can be amiss
When simpleness and duty tender it.

Midsummer Night's Dream 5.1.82–3

In nature there's no blemish but the mind:
None can be called deformed but the unkind.
Virtue is beauty.

Twelfth Night 3.4.366–8

Virtue finds no friends.

Henry VIII 3.1.126

While we do admire
This virtue and this moral discipline,
Let's be no stoics nor no stocks, I pray.

Taming of the Shrew 1.1.29–31

Dost thou think because thou art virtuous,
there shall be no more cakes and ale?

Twelfth Night 2.3.113–14

TRUTH AND LIES

Tell truth, and shame the devil.

1 Henry IV 3.1.55

Truth is truth
To th'end of reck'ning.

Measure for Measure 5.1.48–9

Truth will come to light . . . in the end truth will out.

Merchant of Venice 2.2.76–7

Every man has his fault, and honesty is his.

Timon of Athens 3.1.29–30

Though I am not naturally honest,
I am so sometimes by chance.

Winter's Tale 4.4.714–15

Give me leave to tell you you lie in your throat.

2 Henry IV 1.2.84–5

Let me have no lying: it becomes none but tradesmen.

Winter's Tale 4.4.724–5

Detested kite, thou liest.

King Lear 1.4.254

CONSCIENCE AND REGRET

A peace above all earthly dignities,
A still and quiet conscience.

Henry VIII 3.2.379–80

Disputation
'Tween frozen conscience and hot burning will.

Lucrece 246–7

Some certain dregs of conscience are yet within me.

Richard III 1.4.120–1

'Tis one thing to be tempted, . . .
Another thing to fall.

Measure for Measure 2.1.17–18

What our contempts doth often hurl from us
We wish it ours again.

Antony and Cleopatra 1.2.128–9

Th'offender's sorrow lends but weak relief
To him that bears the strong offence's loss.

Sonnet 34

This momentary joy breeds months of pain;
This hot desire converts to cold disdain.

Lucrece 690–1

I wasted time, and now doth time waste me.

Richard II 5.5.49

I have not kept my square, but that to come
Shall all be done by th' rule.

Antony and Cleopatra 2.3.6–7

It is the purpose that makes strong the vow.

Troilus and Cressida 5.3.23

What we do determine, oft we break.
Purpose is but the slave to memory.

Hamlet 3.2.189–90

His promises were as he then was, mighty:
But his performance, as he is now, nothing.

Henry VIII 4.2.41–2

Bad Habits

Refrain tonight,
And that shall lend a kind of easiness
To the next abstinence, the next more easy;
For use almost can change the stamp of nature.

Hamlet 3.4.167–70

CHIEF JUSTICE Your means are very slender, and your
   waste is great.
FALSTAFF I would it were otherwise, I would my
   means were greater and my waist slenderer.

2 Henry IV 1.2.140–3

I can get no remedy against this consumption of the
purse; borrowing only lingers and lingers it out,
   but the disease is incurable.

2 Henry IV 1.2.236–8

ANXIETY AND FEAR

O polished perturbation! golden care!
That keep'st the ports of slumber open wide
To many a watchful night!

2 Henry IV 4.5.22–4

Doubting things go ill often hurts more
Than to be sure they do.

Cymbeline 1.7.95–6

Care is no cure, but rather corrosive,
For things that are not to be remedied.

1 Henry VI 3.3.3–4

Be not afraid of shadows.

Richard III 5.3.216

Each substance of a grief hath twenty shadows,
Which shows like grief itself.

Richard II 2.2.14–15

Extreme fear can neither fight nor fly.

Lucrece 230

To be furious
Is to be frighted out of fear.

Antony and Cleopatra 3.13.200–1

In time we hate that which we often fear.

Antony and Cleopatra 1.3.13

HOPE

The tender leaves of hopes.

Henry VIII 3.2.353

The miserable have no other medicine
But only hope.

Measure for Measure 3.1.2–3

Let us not burden our remembrances with
A heaviness that's gone.

Tempest 5.1.200–1

There is a world elsewhere!

Coriolanus 3.3.135

HAPPINESS

There was a star danced, and under that was I born.

Much Ado About Nothing 2.1.316

As merry as crickets.

1 Henry IV 2.4.88

As merry as the day is long.

Much Ado About Nothing 2.1.45

My crown is called content;
A crown it is that seldom kings enjoy.

3 Henry VI 3.1.64–5

'Tis a lucky day, boy, and we'll do good deeds on 't.

Winter's Tale 3.3.133–4

[25]

LOVE

If thou remember'st not the slightest folly
That ever love did make thee run into,
Thou hast not loved.

As You Like It 2.4.32–4

Love is blind, and lovers cannot see
The pretty follies that themselves commit.

Merchant of Venice 2.6.6–7

Eternal love . . .
Weighs not the dust and injury of age.

Sonnet 108

This Earthly World

ADVICE

The fool doth think he is wise, but the wiseman knows himself
to be a fool.

As You Like It 5.1.30–1

Love all, trust a few,
Do wrong to none. Be able for thine enemy
Rather in power than use, and keep thy friend
Under thy own life's key.

All's Well That Ends Well 1.1.63–6

Have more than thou showest,
Speak less than thou knowest,
Lend less than thou owest.

King Lear 1.4.116–18

These few precepts in thy memory
Look thou character. Give thy thoughts no tongue,
Nor any unproportioned thought his act.
Be thou familiar, but by no means vulgar;
Those friends thou hast, and their adoption tried,
Grapple them unto thy soul with hoops of steel,
But do not dull thy palm with entertainment
Of each new-hatched, unfledged courage. Beware
Of entrance to a quarrel, but being in,
Bear't that th'opposed may beware of thee.
Give every man thy ear, but few thy voice;
Take each man's censure, but reserve thy judgment.
Costly thy habit as thy purse can buy,
But not expressed in fancy; rich, not gaudy;
For the apparel oft proclaims the man, . . .
Neither a borrower nor a lender be,
For loan oft loses both itself and friend,
And borrowing dulls the edge of husbandry.
This above all: to thine own self be true,
And it must follow as the night the day
Thou canst not then be false to any man.

Hamlet 1.3.58–72, 75–80

When we mean to build,
We first survey the plot, then draw the model,
And when we see the figure of the house,
Then must we rate the cost of the erection,
Which if we find outweighs ability,
What do we then but draw anew the model
In fewer offices, or at least desist
To build at all?

2 Henry IV 1.3.41–8

Wisely and slow; they stumble that run fast.

Romeo and Juliet 2.3.90

Striving to better, oft we mar what's well.

King Lear 1.4.342

Better a little chiding than a great deal of heartbreak.

Merry Wives of Windsor 5.3.9–10

    Men
Can counsel and speak comfort to that grief
Which they themselves not feel; but tasting it,
Their counsel turns to passion.

Much Ado About Nothing 5.1.20–3

Do not as some ungracious pastors do,
Show me the steep and thorny way to heaven,
Whiles like a puffed and reckless libertine
Himself the primrose path of dalliance treads,
And recks not his own rede.

Hamlet 1.3.47–51

OUR FRIENDS

Keep thy friend
Under thy own life's key.

All's Well That Ends Well 1.1.65–6

Those friends thou hast, and their adoption tried,
Grapple them unto thy soul with hoops of steel.

Hamlet 1.3.62–3

A friend should bear his friend's infirmities.

Julius Caesar 4.3.85

I count myself in nothing else so happy
As in a soul remembering my good friends.

Richard II 2.3.46–7

There's no more faith in thee than in a stewed prune.

1 Henry IV 3.3.112–13

I knew what you would prove. My friends told me as
much, and I thought no less.

As You Like It 4.1.174–6

Friendship is constant in all other things
Save in the office and affairs of love.

Much Ado About Nothing 2.1.166–7

The private wound is deepest.

Two Gentlemen of Verona 5.4.71

Work and Play

To business that we love we rise betime
And go to't with delight.

Antony and Cleopatra 4.4.20–1

Since I received command to do this business
I have not slept one wink.

Cymbeline 3.4.99–100

Thou art not for the fashion of these times,
Where none will sweat but for promotion.

As You Like It 2.3.59–60

'Remuneration'! O, that's the Latin word
for three farthings.

Love's Labour's Lost 3.1.133–4

Experience is by industry achieved,
And perfected by the swift course of time.

Two Gentlemen of Verona 1.3.22–3

Perseverance, dear my lord,
Keeps honour bright.

Troilus and Cressida 3.3.152–3

If it be man's work, I'll do't.

King Lear 5.3.40

My nature is subdued
To what it works in, like the dyer's hand.

Sonnet III

I were better to be eaten to death with a rust
than to be scoured to nothing with perpetual motion.

2 Henry IV 1.2.218–20

These are barren tasks, too hard to keep:
Not to see ladies, study, fast, not sleep.

Love's Labour's Lost 1.1.47–8

Celerity is never more admired
Than by the negligent.

Antony and Cleopatra 3.7.24–5

Cudgel thy brains no more about it.

Hamlet 5.1.56

ACTION AND DELAY

Action is eloquence.

Coriolanus 3.2.76

Boldness be my friend!

Cymbeline 1.7.18

Confident against the world in arms.

1 Henry IV 5.1.117

Imitate the action of the tiger:
Stiffen up the sinews, conjure up the blood.

Henry V 3.1.6–7

All things are ready, if our minds be so.

Henry V 4.3.71

That we would do,
We should do when we would.

Hamlet 4.7.118–19

PORTIA Good sentences, and well pronounced.
NERISSA They would be better if well followed.

Merchant of Venice 1.2.10–11

Talkers are no good doers.

Richard III 1.3.351

Letting 'I dare not' wait upon 'I would,'
Like the poor cat i'th' adage.

Macbeth 1.7.44–5

Advantage feeds him fat while men delay.

1 Henry IV 3.2.180

Dull not device by coldness and delay!

Othello 2.3.376

The excuse that thou dost make in this delay
Is longer than the tale thou dost excuse.

Romeo and Juliet 2.5.33–4

I do but dream on sovereignty;
Like one that stands upon a promontory
And spies a far-off shore where he would tread.

3 Henry VI 3.2.134–6

Be not afraid of greatness. Some are born great,
some achieve greatness, and some have greatness
thrust upon 'em.

Twelfth Night 2.5.139–41

No man's pie is freed
From his ambitious finger.

Henry VIII 1.1.52–3

Vaulting ambition, which o'erleaps itself.

Macbeth 1.7.27

Lowliness is young ambition's ladder
Whereto the climber upward turns his face;
But when he once attains the upmost round
He then unto the ladder turns his back,
Looks in the clouds, scorning the base degrees
By which he did ascend.

Julius Caesar 2.1.22–7

Ambition should be made of sterner stuff.

Julius Caesar 3.2.93

Oft expectation fails, and most oft there
Where most it promises.

All's Well That Ends Well 2.1.141–2

We are not the first
Who with best meaning have incurred the worst.

King Lear 5.3.3–4

MACBETH If we should fail?
LADY MACBETH We fail?
But screw your courage to the sticking-place,
And we'll not fail.

Macbeth 1.7.59–62

How my achievements mock me!

Troilus and Cressida 4.2.71

The Way of the World

O how full of briers is this working-day world!

As You Like It 1.3.11–12

The world is not thy friend, nor the world's law;
The world affords no law to make thee rich.

Romeo and Juliet 5.1.72–3

Honours thrive
When rather from our acts we them derive
Than our foregoers.

All's Well That Ends Well 2.3.136–8

Ye have angels' faces, but heaven knows your hearts.

Henry VIII 3.1.145

'Tis better to be lowly born
And range with humble livers in content
Than to be perked up in a glistering grief
And wear a golden sorrow.

Henry VIII 2.3.19–22

That glib and oily art
To speak and purpose not.

King Lear 1.1.226–7

There's no art
To find the mind's construction in the face:
He was a gentleman on whom I built
An absolute trust.

Macbeth 1.4.11–14

He that loves to be flattered is worthy o'th' flatterer.

Timon of Athens 1.1.229–30

New-made honour doth forget men's names.

King John 1.1.187

Who so firm that cannot be seduced?

Julius Caesar 1.2.311

In the corrupted currents of this world
Offence's gilded hand may shove by justice,
And oft 'tis seen the wicked prize itself
Buys out the law.

Hamlet 3.3.57–60

Life and Time

There's a divinity that shapes our ends,
Rough-hew them how we will.

Hamlet 5.2.10–11

    The slaves of chance, and flies
Of every wind that blows.

Winter's Tale 4.4.542–3

My stars shine darkly over me.

Twelfth Night 2.1.3–4

Then I defy you, stars!

Romeo and Juliet 5.1.24

Our remedies oft in ourselves do lie
Which we ascribe to heaven.

All's Well That Ends Well 1.1.216–17

The fault, dear Brutus, is not in our stars
But in ourselves, that we are underlings.

Julius Caesar 1.2.139–40

The web of our life is of a mingled yarn,
good and ill together.

All's Well That Ends Well 4.3.68–9

Life's uncertain voyage.

Timon of Athens 5.1.202

This world to me is as a lasting storm.

Pericles 4.1.19

Life's but a walking shadow; a poor player,
That struts and frets his hour upon the stage,
And then is heard no more: it is a tale
Told by an idiot, full of sound and fury,
Signifying nothing.

Macbeth 5.5.24–8

Time hath, my lord, a wallet at his back,
Wherein he puts alms for oblivion,
A great-sized monster of ingratitudes.
Those scraps are good deeds past, which are
Devoured as fast as they are made, forgot
As soon as done.

Troilus and Cressida 3.3.147–52

Like as the waves make towards the pebbled shore,
So do our minutes hasten to their end.

Sonnet 60

We are such stuff
As dreams are made on, and our little life
Is rounded with a sleep.

Tempest 4.1.156–8